Common Core
Standards Practice
Workbook

Grade K

ISBN-13: 978-0-328-75683-4
ISBN-10:   0-328-75683-0
20 2021

KIndergarten Contents

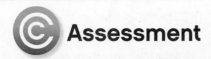 **Standards Practice**

Assessment

About this Workbook

Savvas is pleased to offer this **Common Core Standards Practice Workbook**. In it, you will find pages to help you become good math thinkers and problem-solvers. It includes these pages:

- **Common Core Standards Practice pages.** For each Common Core Standard, you will find two pages of practice exercises. On these pages, you will find different kinds of exercises that are similar to the items expected to be on the end-of-year assessments you will be taking starting in Grade 3.

- **Practice for the Common Core Assessment.** You will find a practice assessment, similar to the Next Generation Assessment that you will be taking starting in Grade 3. The Practice End-of-Year Assessment has 30 items that are all aligned to the Common Core Standards for Mathematical Content.

Common Core Standards Practice

K.CC.A.1 Count to 100 by ones and by tens.

 1

| 1 | 2 | 3 | 4 | _____ |

2

| 29 | 30 | 31 | 32 | _____ |

3

| 66 | 67 | 68 | 69 | _____ |

To the Teacher: Read the items below aloud to children.
1 – **3** What number comes next? Write the number in the empty box.

CC1

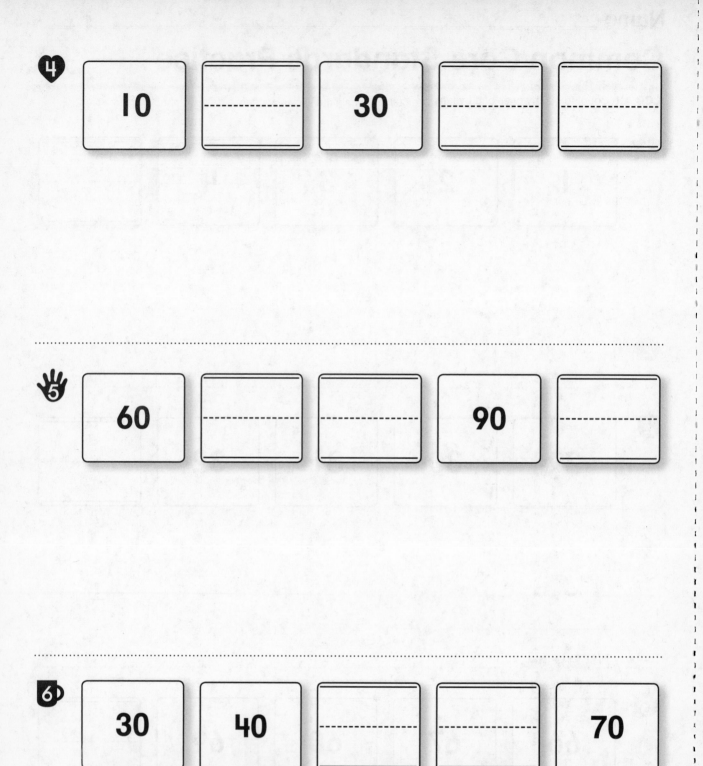

4 | 10 | ___ | 30 | ___ | ___ |

5 | 60 | ___ | ___ | 90 | ___ |

6 | 30 | 40 | ___ | ___ | 70 |

To the Teacher: Read the items below aloud to children.

4 – 6 Count by 10s. What number comes next? Write the number in the empty box.

Name _____

Common Core Standards Practice

K.CC.A.2 Count forward beginning from a given number within the known sequence (instead of having to begin at 1).

 1

| 12 | 13 | 14 | ------ | ------ |

2

| 77 | 78 | 79 | ------ |

3

| 63 | 64 | ------ |

4

| 54 | 55 | ------ |

To the Teacher: Read the items below aloud to children.

1 – 4 What number comes next? Write the number in the empty box.

CC 3

5 | 21 | 22 | 23 | ____ | ____ |

6 | 47 | 48 | 49 | ____ | ____ |

7 | 53 | 54 | ____ | 56 | ____ |

8 | 61 | ____ | ____ | 64 | ____ |

To the Teacher: Read the items below aloud to children.

5 – 8 What number comes next? Write the number in the empty box.

CC 4

Name _____

Common Core Standards Practice

K.CC.A.3 Write numbers from 0 to 20. Represent a number of objects with a written numeral 0–20 (with 0 representing a count of no objects).

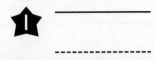 _____
- - - - - - - - - - - - - - -
_____

 _____
- - - - - - - - - - - - - - -
_____

❸ _____
- - - - - - - - - - - - - - -
_____

❤ _____
- - - - - - - - - - - - - - -
_____

To the Teacher: Read the items below aloud to children.
⭐ Write the number 8 on the line.
🍎 Write the number 13 on the line.
◀ Write the number 9 on the line.
❤ Write the number 16 on the line.

Name

Common Core Standards Practice

✋⁵

_____

_____

✍⁶

_____

_____

To the Teacher: Read the directions for each item aloud to children.
✋⁵ How many cubes are there? Count the cubes and write the number on the line.
✍⁶ How many apples are there? Count the apples and write the number on the line.

Name _____

Common Core Standards Practice

K.CC.B.4a Understand the relationship between numbers and quantities; connect counting to cardinality. When counting objects, say the number names in the standard order, pairing each object with one and only one number name and each number name with one and only one object.

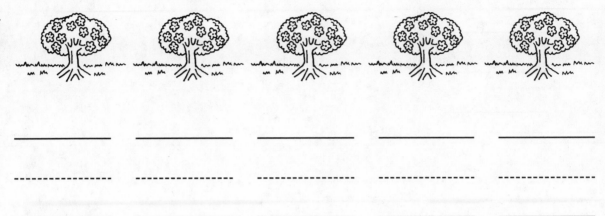

_____ _____ _____ _____ _____

- - - - - - - - - -   - - - - - - - - - -   - - - - - - - - - -   - - - - - - - - - -   - - - - - - - - - -

_____ _____ _____ _____ _____

_____ _____ _____ _____ _____ _____ _____ _____

- - - - -   - - - - -   - - - - -   - - - - -   - - - - -   - - - - -   - - - - -   - - - - -

_____ _____ _____ _____ _____ _____ _____ _____

To the Teacher: Read the directions for each item aloud to children.
⭐ Look at the trees. Count the trees and write the number that you say on the line below each tree.
② Look at the apples. Count the apples and write the number that you say on the line below each apple.

3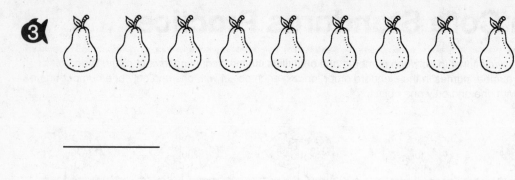

_____

- - - - - - - - -

_____

4

_____   _____

- - - - - - - - -   - - - - - - - - -

_____   _____

To the Teacher: Read the directions for each item aloud to children.

3 Count the pears. On the line, write how many pears you counted.

4 Count the cars in the first box. On the line, write how many cars you counted. Then count the cars in the second box. On the line, write how many cars you counted. Which box has more cars? (Children should notice that both boxes have the same number of cars.)

Common Core Standards Practice

K.CC.B.4c Understand the relationship between numbers and quantities; connect counting to cardinality. Understand that each successive number name refers to a quantity that is one larger.

1 14   15

2 20   19

3 33   34

To the Teacher: Read the directions for each item aloud to children.
1 – **3** Look at the two numbers. Which number is greater? Circle the number that is greater.

4 40   41

5 50   49

6 88   89

To the Teacher: Read the directions for each item aloud to children.
4 – 6 Look at the two numbers. Which number is greater? Circle the number that is greater.

CC 10

Name _____

Common Core Standards Practice

K.CC.B.5 Count to answer "how many?" questions about as many as 20 things arranged in a line, a rectangular array, or a circle, or as many as 10 things in a scattered configuration; given a number from 1–20, count out that many objects.

1

_____

- - - - - - - - - - - - - - -

_____

2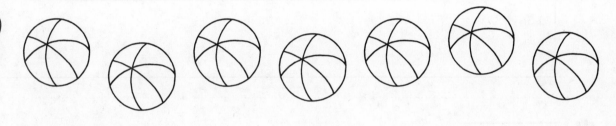

_____

- - - - - - - - - - - - - - -

_____

3

_____

- - - - - - - - - - - - - - -

_____

To the Teacher: Read the directions for each item aloud to children.
1 How many carrots are there? Count the carrots and write the number on the line.
2 How many balls are there? Count the balls and write the number on the line.
3 How many plants are there? Count the plants and write the number on the line.

CC 11

4 _____

_____

[box]

....

5 _____

_____

[box]

To the Teacher: Read the directions for each item aloud to children.

4 Write the number 11 on the line. Then draw 11 circles in the box.

5 Write the number 15 on the line. Then draw 15 squares in the box.

Name _____

Common Core Standards Practice

K.CC.C.6 Identify whether the number of objects in one group is greater than, less than, or equal to the number of objects in another group, e.g., by using matching and counting strategies.

To the Teacher: Read the directions for each item aloud to children.

⭐ Are there more strawberries or peaches? Match each strawberry to one peach. Draw a line from one strawberry to one peach. Did you match all of the strawberries? (Yes) Did you match all of the peaches? (No). Circle the fruit that has more.

🍎 Are there more puppies or dishes? Match each puppy to one dish. Draw a line from one puppy to one dish. Did you match all of the puppies? (No) Did you match all of the dishes? (Yes). Circle the picture that has fewer.

3

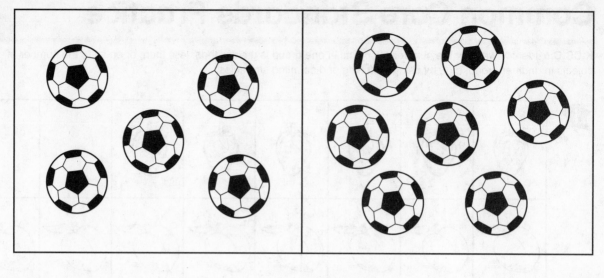

_____   _____

- - - - - - - - -   - - - - - - - - -

_____   _____

4

To the Teacher: Read the directions for each item aloud to children.

3 Count the balls in each box. Write the number below each box. Which box has fewer balls? Circle the box that has fewer balls.

4 Match each bird to one nest. Are there more birds or nests? Circle the picture that has more.

CC 14

Name _____

Common Core Standards Practice

K.CC.C.7 Compare two numbers between 1 and 10 presented as written numerals.

 1   6

2 4   3

3 7   10

To the Teacher: Read the directions for each item aloud to children.
1 Which number is greater? Circle the number that is greater.
2 Which number is less? Circle the number that is less.
3 Which number is greater? Circle the number that is greater.

CC 15

4 9   5

5 8   2

6 5   1

To the Teacher: Read the directions for each item aloud to children.
4 Which number is less? Circle the number that is less.
5 Which number is greater? Circle the number that is greater.
6 Which number is less? Circle the number that is less.

CC 16

Name _____

Common Core Standards Practice

K.OA.A.1 Represent addition and subtraction with objects, fingers, mental images, drawings, sounds (e.g., claps), acting out situations, verbal explanations, expressions, or equations.

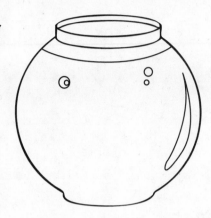

_____

_____

_____

_____

To the Teacher: Read the items below aloud to children.

⭐ Jana has 3 fish and Ara has 5 fish. Draw Jana's fish in the first bowl and Ara's fish in the second bowl. How many fish did you draw? Write that number on the line.

🍎 Hanna put 3 flowers in the pot. Then she put 4 more flowers in the pot. Draw Hanna's flowers in the pot. Write that number on the line.

CC 17

3

4

Name _____

Common Core Standards Practice

K.OA.A.2 Solve addition and subtraction word problems, and add and subtract within 10, e.g., by using objects or drawings to represent the problem.

1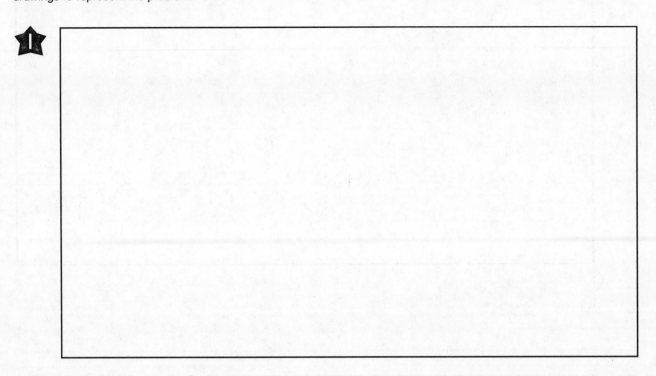

2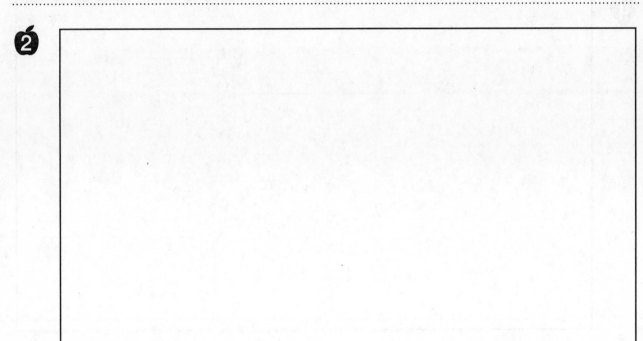

To the Teacher: Read the items below aloud to children.
⭐ Hayley has 6 bows. Her sister has 3 bows. How many bows do Hayley and her sister have? Show the answer in the box. Use numbers or drawings.
🍎 William has 5 footballs. He gives 2 footballs to his friends. How many footballs does he have now? Show the answer in the box. Use numbers or drawings.

3

4

To the Teacher: Read the items below aloud to children.

3 Aida has 7 beads. Her mother gives her 4 more beads. Show all of Aida's beads in the box. Use numbers or drawings.

4 Frieda sees 5 stars in the sky. Then she sees 4 more stars. Show all of the stars Frieda sees in the box. Use numbers or drawings.

CC 20

Name _____

Common Core Standards Practice

K.OA.A.3 Decompose numbers less than or equal to 10 into pairs in more than one way, e.g., by using objects or drawings, and record each decomposition by a drawing or equation (e.g., 5 = 2 + 3 and 5 = 4 + 1).

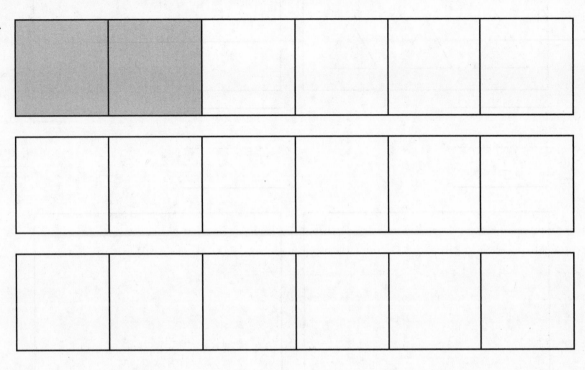

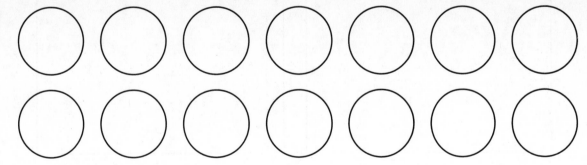

To the Teacher: Read the items below aloud to children.
⭐ Look at the first row of boxes. How many boxes are there? (6) How many are shaded? (2) How many are not shaded? (4) 2 and 4 make 6. Color some boxes in green and some in yellow to show two other ways to make 6.
❷ Look at the row of circles. How many circles are there? (7) Color some circles in red and some circles in blue to show two ways to make 7.

To the Teacher: Read the items below aloud to children.

3 Look at the triangles. How many triangles are in the first box? (6) How many are in the second box? (3) How many triangles are there in all? (9). Show two other ways to make 9.

Common Core Standards Practice

K.OA.A.4 For any number from 1 to 9, find the number that makes 10 when added to the given number, e.g., by using objects or drawings, and record the answer with a drawing or equation.

_____

- - - - - - - - - - - -

4 + _____

- -

_____

- - - - - - - - - - - -

5 + _____

To the Teacher: Read the items below aloud to children.

⭐ Look at the hats. How many hats are there? (4) How many more do you need to make 10? Draw that many hats. Write the number of hats that you drew on the line.

❷ Look at the crowns. How many crowns are there? How many more do you need to make 10? Draw that many crowns. Write the number of hats that you drew on the line.

3

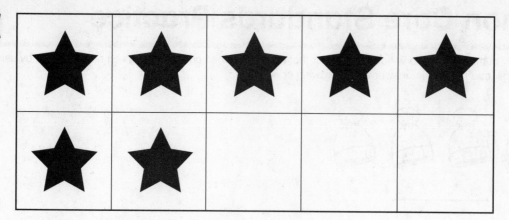

_____

7 + _____

4

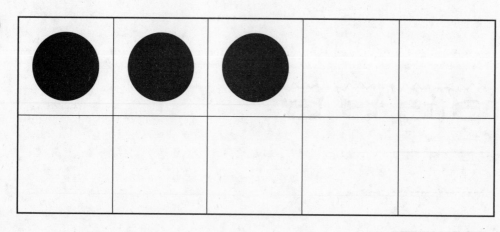

_____

3 + _____

To the Teacher: Read the items below aloud to children.
3 Look at the stars in the ten-frame. How many more stars do you need to make 10? Draw that many stars.
Write the number of stars you drew on the line.
4 Look at the counters in the ten-frame. How many more counters do you need to make 10? Draw that many counters.
Write the number of counters you drew on the line.

CC 24

Name _____

Common Core Standards Practice

K.OA.A.5 Fluently add and subtract within 5.

⭐ **1**   1 + 4 = _____

🍎 **2**   3 − 2 = _____

3   3 + 1 = _____

❤️ **4**   4 − 2 = _____

✋ **5**   3 + 2 = _____

☕ **6**   4 − 3 = _____

To the Teacher: Read the items below aloud to children.

1, **3**, **5** Find the sum.

2, **4**, **6** Find the difference.

7 1 + 2 = _____

8 4 − 1 = _____

9 1 + 1 = _____

10 3 − 1 = _____

11 2 + 2 = _____

12 2 − 1 = _____

To the Teacher: Read the items below aloud to children.

7, **9**, **11** Find the sum.

8, **10**, **12** Find the difference.

CC 26

Name _____

Common Core Standards Practice

K.NBT.A.1 Compose and decompose numbers from 11 to 19 into ten ones and some further ones, e.g., by using objects or drawings, and record each composition or decomposition by a drawing or equation (such as 18 = 10 + 8); understand that these numbers are composed of ten ones and one, two, three, four, five, six, seven, eight, or nine ones.

⭐ **1**

14

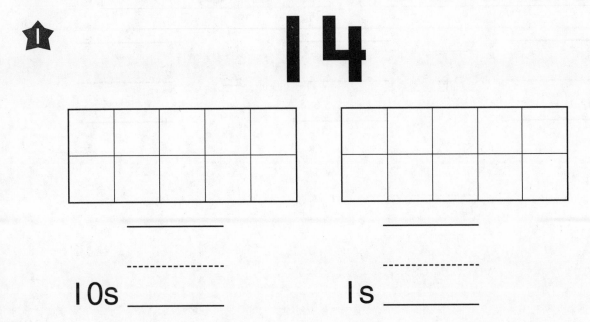

_____   _____

10s _____   1s _____

🍎 **2**

17

_____   _____

10s _____   1s _____

To the Teacher: Read the items below aloud to children.

⭐ Draw circles in the ten-frames to show 14. How many 10s are in 14? Write the number on the line. How many 1s? Write the number on the line.

🍎 Draw circles in the ten-frames to show 17. How many 10s are in 17? Write the number on the line. How many 1s? Write the number on the line.

CC 27

3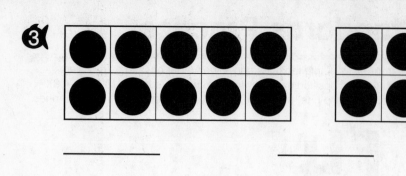

_____   +   _____   =   _____

------------   ------------   ------------

_____   _____   _____

4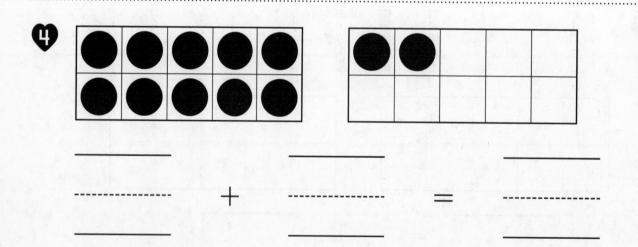

_____   +   _____   =   _____

------------   ------------   ------------

_____   _____   _____

To the Teacher: Read the items below aloud to children.
3 Look at the ten-frames. What number do they show? Write the numbers on the lines.
4 Look at the ten-frames. What number do they show? Write the numbers on the lines.

Name _____

Common Core Standards Practice

K.MD.A.1 Describe measurable attributes of objects, such as length or weight. Describe several measurable attributes of a single object.

 1

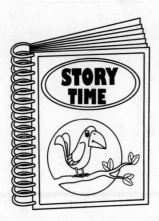

STORY
TIME

---

 2   Yes   No

---

3   Yes   No

---

4   Yes   No

To the Teacher: Read the items below aloud to children.

★ Look at the book. Maya needs to measure the height. Which side should she measure to find the height?
Draw a green line next to the height. She will also measure the width. Which side should she measure to find the width?
Draw a blue line next to the width.

2 Can you measure the weight of a pencil? Circle Yes or No.

3 Can you measure the length of an eraser? Circle Yes or No.

4 Can you measure the height of a plant? Circle Yes or No.

CC 29

5 Yes   No

6 Yes   No

7 Yes   No

8 Yes   No

To the Teacher: Read the items below aloud to children.
5 Can you measure the weight of a dog? Circle Yes or No.
6 Can you measure the length of a dog? Circle Yes or No.
7 Can you measure the height of a dog? Circle Yes or No.
8 Can you measure the width of a dog? Circle Yes or No.

Name _____

Common Core Standards Practice

K.MD.A.2 Directly compare two objects with a measurable attribute in common, to see which object has "more of"/"less of" the attribute, and describe the difference.

⭐**1**

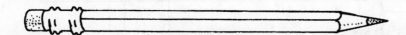

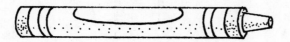

🍎**2**

To the Teacher: Read the items below aloud to children.
⭐ Look at the pencil and the crayon. Which is longer? Draw a circle around the one that is longer.
🍎 Look at the tree and the bush. Which is shorter? Draw a circle around the one that is shorter.

To the Teacher: Read the items below aloud to children.

❸ Look at the chair and the couch. Which is wider? Draw a line under the one that is wider.

❹ Look at the car and the bicycle. Which is lighter? Draw a line under the one that is lighter.

Common Core Standards Practice

K.MD.B.3 Classify objects into given categories; count the numbers of objects in each category and sort the categories by count.

⭐ 1

_____

- - - - - - - - - -

_____

🍎 2

Shoes	Hats

_____   _____

- - - - - - - - - -   - - - - - - - - - -

_____   _____

To the Teacher: Read the items below aloud to children.

⭐ Look at the objects. How can you sort the objects? Put a circle around all of the animals. How many animals are in the group? Write the number on the line.

🍎 Look at the table. Paolo put the shoes in one group and the hats in another group. Count the shoes in the group. Write the number on the line below the shoes. Count the hats in the group. Write the number on the line below the hats.

CC 33

Balls	Fruit	Shapes

_____

- -

_____

_____

- -

_____

To the Teacher: Read the items below aloud to children.

3 Look at the table. Misha sorts the objects into three groups. Which group has the most objects? Write the name of the group on the first line. Which group has the fewest? Write the name of the group on the second line.

CC 34

Name _____

Common Core Standards Practice

K.G.A.1 Describe objects in the environment using names of shapes, and describe the relative positions of these objects using terms such as *above, below, beside, in front of, behind,* and *next to.*

To the Teacher: Read the items below aloud to children.

⭐ Look at the house. Find all of the squares and color them.

🍎 Look at the classroom. Find all of the rectangles and color them.

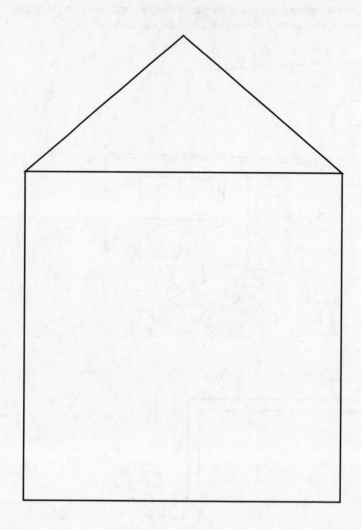

To the Teacher: Read the items below aloud to children.

3 Look at the house. Draw a rectangle in front of the house. Color it brown. Then draw a circle above the house. Color it yellow. Draw a triangle next to the house. Color it green. Draw a square beside the green triangle and color it blue.

Name _____

Common Core Standards Practice

K.G.A.2 Correctly name shapes regardless of their orientations or overall size.

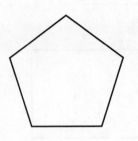  

 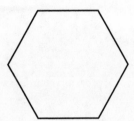 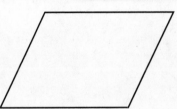

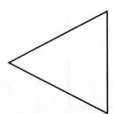 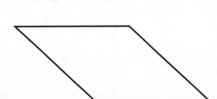 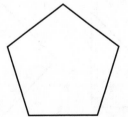

To the Teacher: Read the items below aloud to children.

⭐ Look at the shapes. Which is a rectangle? Put a circle around the rectangles.

🍎 Look at the shape next to number 2. Then look at the shapes below. Put an X on the shape that is the same.

3

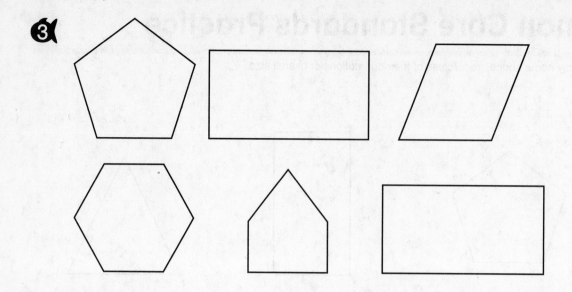

4

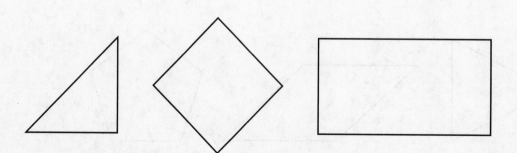

To the Teacher: Read the items below aloud to children.

3 Look at the shapes. Find all of the pentagons and color them.

4 Look at the shape next to number 4. Then look at the shapes below. Put an X on the shape that is the same.

CC 38

Name _____

Common Core Standards Practice

K.G.A.3 Identify shapes as two-dimensional (lying in a plane, "flat") or three-dimensional ("solid").

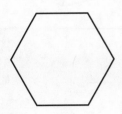 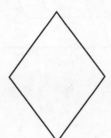 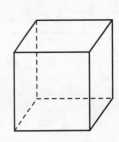

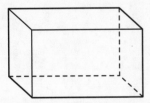 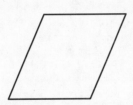 

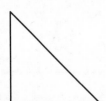 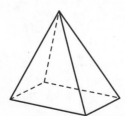 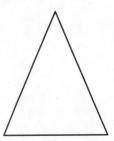

To the Teacher: Read the items below aloud to children.
⭐ Look at the shapes. Find all of the shapes that are flat. Color all of the flat shapes green.

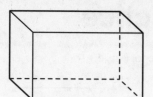  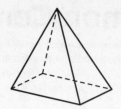

 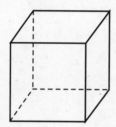 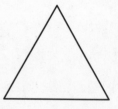

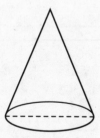 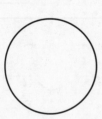 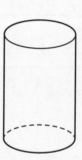

To the Teacher: Read the items below aloud to children.

❷ Look at the shapes. Find all of the shapes that are solids and put a circle around them.

CC 40

Name _____

Common Core Standards Practice

K.G.B.4 Analyze and compare two- and three-dimensional shapes, in different sizes and orientations, using informal language to describe their similarities, differences, parts (e.g., number of sides and vertices/"corners") and other attributes (e.g., having sides of equal length).

 1

 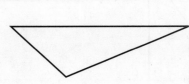 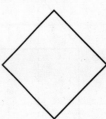

 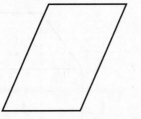 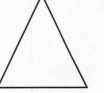 

2

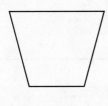 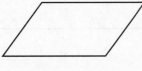 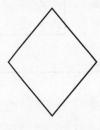

_____   _____   _____

- - - - - - - - -   - - - - - - - - -   - - - - - - - - -

_____   _____   _____

 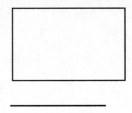

_____   _____   _____

- - - - - - - - -   - - - - - - - - -   - - - - - - - - -

_____   _____   _____

To the Teacher: Read the items below aloud to children.

1 Look at the shapes. Circle all of the shapes that have three corners.

2 Look at the shapes. Count the sides of each shape. How many sides does each shape have? Write that number on the line below each shape. How are the shapes the same? (They have the same number of sides.)

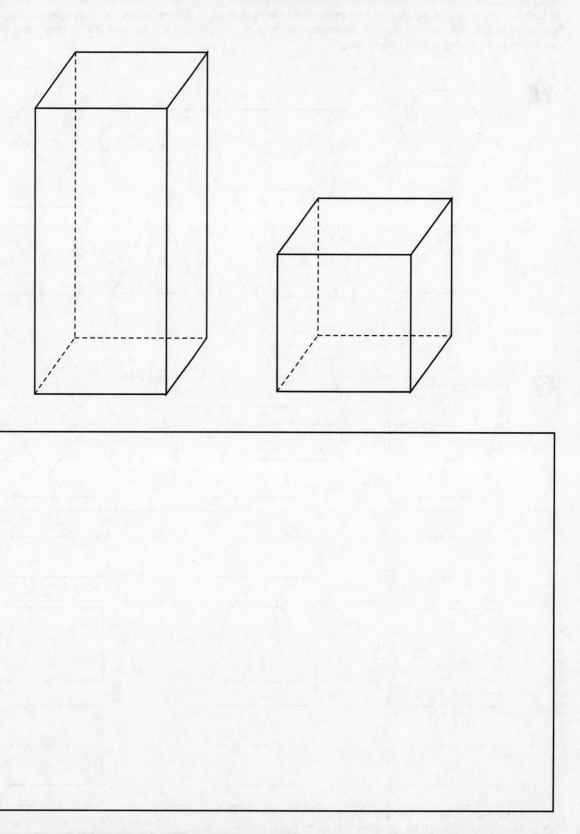

To the Teacher: Read the items below aloud to children.

3 Look at the two solids. Tell how they are the same. Tell how they are different. You can use words or pictures.

Name _____

Common Core Standards Practice

K.G.B.5 Model shapes in the world by building shapes from components (e.g., sticks and clay balls) and drawing shapes.

....

To the Teacher: Read the items below aloud to children.

 Draw a triangle. Make the two sides the same length.

 Draw a rectangle.

To the Teacher: Read the items below aloud to children.

3 Draw a hexagon.

4 Draw a square. Then draw a line through it to make two triangles.

CC 44

Name _____

Common Core Standards Practice

K.G.B.6 Compose simple shapes to form larger shapes.

 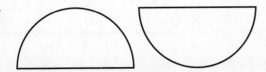

....

To the Teacher: Read the items below aloud to children.
⭐ Look at these shapes. What new shape can you make if you put them together? Draw that new shape.
🍎 Look at these shapes. What new shape can you make if you put them together? Draw that new shape.

Name

Common Core Standards Practice

3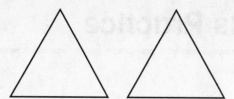

4

To the Teacher: Read the items below aloud to children.
3 Look at these shapes. What new shape can you make if you put them together? Draw that new shape.
4 Look at these shapes. What new shape can you make if you put them together? Draw that new shape.

Practice End-of-Year Assessment

_____

- - - - - - - - - - - - - - - -

_____

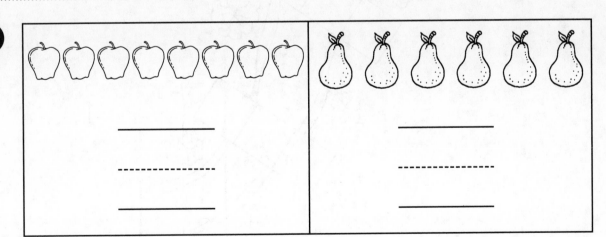

To the Teacher: Read the items below aloud to children.
❶ Look at the cats. There are 10 cats. Write the number on the line.
❷ Count the apples and write the number on the line. Then count the pears and write the number on the line. Are there more apples or pears? Draw a circle around the greater number.

CC 47

3

4

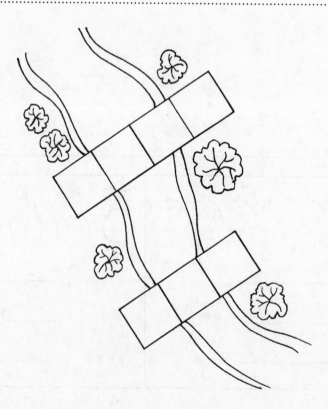

To the Teacher: Read the items below aloud to children.

3 Kate has 8 pretzels. How many more does she need to make 10? Draw more pretzels to make 10.

4 Look at the picture. Can you find a square? Color one square blue.

5

4   7

- -

6

$$3 + 2 = \underline{}$$

- -

7

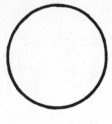 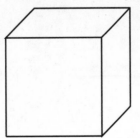

To the Teacher: Read the items below aloud to children.
5 Look at the two numbers. Which is less? Circle the number that is less.
6 Find the sum of the two numbers.
7 Look at the two shapes. Which is a flat shape? Circle the flat shape.

CC 49

8

9

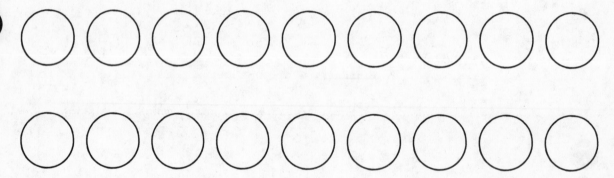

To the Teacher: Read the items below aloud to children.

8 There are two groups of peaches. Which group has more peaches? Circle the group with more peaches.

9 How can you make 9? Show two different ways to make 9. Color some circles blue and the other circles red to show 9.

10

15, 16, 17, ____

11

5   4

12

[empty box]

To the Teacher: Read the items below aloud to children.
10 What number comes next? Write the number that comes next on the line.
11 Look at the two numbers. Which is greater? Circle the number that is greater.
12 Draw a shape that has three sides and three corners.

CC 51

13

14

_____

- - - - - - - - - - - -

_____

To the Teacher: Read the items below aloud to children.

13 Josie had 10 balloons. Three of them popped. Draw the balloons that Josie had. Then show how many popped.

14 A zoo had 3 turtles. Then the zoo got 5 more turtles. How many turtles are in the zoo? Write the number on the line.

15

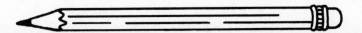

16

_____   _____

- - - - - - -   - - - - - - -

Ten _____   Ones _____

To the Teacher: Read the items below aloud to children.

15 Raul will measure the length of a pencil. Which is the length of the pencil? Draw a line along the length of the pencil.

16 Color in the ten-frames to show 14. How many 10s are there? Write that number on the first line. How many 1s are there? Write that number on the second line.

17

Elizabeth's Stuffed Dogs	Hannah's Stuffed Dogs

18

Circles	Triangles	Squares

_____

- - - - - - - - - - - - - -

_____

To the Teacher: Read the items below aloud to children.

17 Elizabeth has 5 stuffed dogs. Her sister, Hannah has 4 stuffed dogs. Draw circles to show how many stuffed dogs they have.

18 Look at the column with the triangles. How many triangles are in that group? Write the number on the line.

_____

- - - - - - - - - -

_____

To the Teacher: Read the items below aloud to children.

⑲ Look at the frogs. How many are there? Count the frogs and write the number on the line.

⑳ Look at the two bananas. Which one is shorter? Circle the banana that is shorter.

CC 55

21

22

_____

_____

To the Teacher: Read the items below aloud to children.

21 Look at the cherries. How many cherries are there? (7) Use green and blue to color the cherries in the first row to show one way to make 7. Use red and orange to color the cherries in the second row to show another way to make 7.

22 Look at the two plates of muffins. There are 3 muffins on one plate. There are 5 muffins on the other plate. Adam will put all of the muffins on one plate. How many muffins will be on the one plate? Write the number on the line.

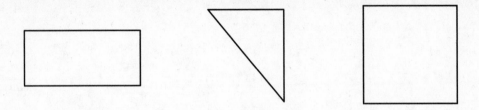

_____   _____

------------ + ------------ = 10

_____   _____

To the Teacher: Read the items below aloud to children.
23 Look at the shapes. Which one is a square? Draw an X on the square.
24 How many cubes are there? Write the number of cubes on the first line. How many more cubes do you need to make 10? Write that number on the second line.

25

26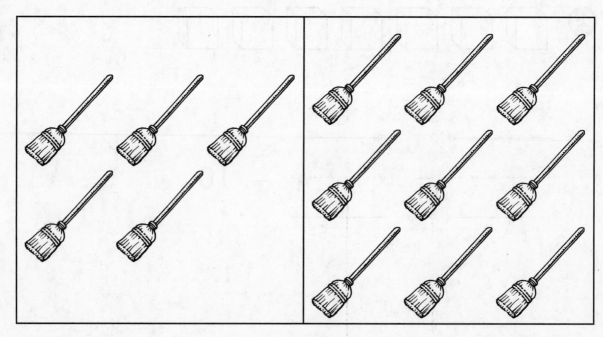

To the Teacher: Read the items below aloud to children.

25 Look at the shapes. What new shape can you make if you put the two shapes together? Draw that shape.

26 Look at the two groups of brooms. Which group has more? Circle the group that has more brooms.

CC 58

27

$$4 - 3 = \underline{}$$

28

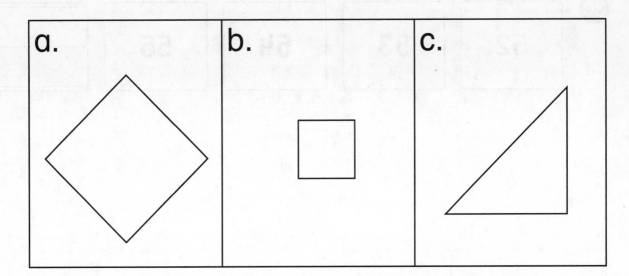

To the Teacher: Read the items below aloud to children.

27 Find the difference.

28 Look at the shape at the top. Which of the shapes below is the same? Circle the shape that is the same.

18

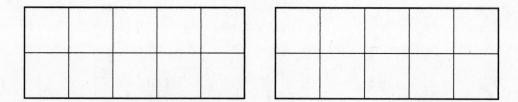

30

52	**53**	**54**	**55**	-------

To the Teacher: Read the items below aloud to children.
29 Look at the number. Color in the two ten-frames to show that number.
30 Read the list of numbers. Write the number that comes next.